YOUR KNOWLEDGE

- We will publish your bachelor's and master's thesis, essays and papers

- Your own eBook and book - sold worldwide in all relevant shops

- Earn money with each sale

Upload your text at www.GRIN.com
and publish for free

Mario Maxwell Müller

How to prepare lesson plans for the Licentiate Music Teaching Programme - T601

GRIN Verlag

Bibliografische Information der Deutschen Nationalbibliothek:

Die Deutsche Bibliothek verzeichnet diese Publikation in der Deutschen National-
bibliografie; detaillierte bibliografische Daten sind im Internet über http://dnb.d-
nb.de/ abrufbar.

Imprint:

Copyright © 2010 GRIN Verlag GmbH
Druck und Bindung: Books on Demand GmbH, Norderstedt Germany
ISBN: 978-3-656-68655-2

This book at GRIN:

http://www.grin.com/en/e-book/273851/how-to-prepare-lesson-plans-for-the-
licentiate-music-teaching-programme

GRIN - Your knowledge has value

Der GRIN Verlag publiziert seit 1998 wissenschaftliche Arbeiten von Studenten, Hochschullehrern und anderen Akademikern als eBook und gedrucktes Buch. Die Verlagswebsite www.grin.com ist die ideale Plattform zur Veröffentlichung von Hausarbeiten, Abschlussarbeiten, wissenschaftlichen Aufsätzen, Dissertationen und Fachbüchern.

Visit us on the internet:

http://www.grin.com/

http://www.facebook.com/grincom

http://www.twitter.com/grin_com

How to prepare lesson plans for the Licentiate Music Teaching Programme

Piano Syllabus (Level 1) – Rock School (UK)

Mario Maxwell Muller - LRSL

T601

Mario Maxwell Müller – Lesson Plan presented for the Qualification: Licentiate in Music Teaching (LRSL) – MUS T601

Notes to the readers:

This book was written for those students preparing for their Rock School Music Teaching Licentiate focussing on the Piano Syllabus for Level 1

In conjunction with the lesson plans please use the Rock School Books (Pitt et al., 2001a, 2001b, 2001c) for Grade 1, Grade 2 and Grade 3 Piano and Keyboard by Simon Pitt, Adrian York and Norton York (2010).

These can be obtained online or through Rock School at the following address:

Rock School
Evergreen House
2 – 4 King Street
Twickenham
Middlesex
TW1 3RZ
Tel: +44 (0) 845 460 4747
Fax: +44 (0) 845460 1960
Email: info@rockschool.co.uk
Website: www.rockschool.co.uk

Assessment is important for any practical lesson to succeed.

- Students are advised to have Log Book with homework assigned regularly
- To give feedback on progress to the parents about their instrumental lessons
- To encourage students to prepare themselves adequately for their practical examination
- I have included an example of practice log book as well for your use

The above lesson will encourage self discipline and aural development. Active participation is crucial for the development of skills as outlined in the Aims and Objectives and highlighted in the Lesson Plan. Homework will be assigned – see Log Book.

**Mario Maxwell Müller – Lesson Plan presented for the Qualification:
Licentiate in Music Teaching (LRSL) – MUS T601**

<u>Dedication</u>

This is written for my late mother, Eileen Theresa Müller, a senior music lecturer at Dower Training College of Education in Port Elizabeth, who died suddenly of endometrial cancer on the 30th December 2009 and the late memory of my dear friend, Franco Giannacarro. My mother inspired me in music so much over the years, from my first piano lesson at the age of 6 to my taking up cello at 13. Upon my return to South Africa from living abroad in Israel I continued with my music education at the University of Port Elizabeth, the same University at which she completed her degree and post graduate studies during the years of Apartheid. Her grace and presence will always fill my heart with joy, as I cherish all the musical moments we shared together.

<u>Acknowledgments</u>

Firstly I would like to thank Rockie Siew, whose support and motivation over the past two years has inspired me to contribute my best at all times. Thank you for your encouragement during my post-graduate studies at Rock School. Secondly I thank my family in South Africa, my father, Douglas Müller, my brother, Damian Charles Müller, and my sister Darleen Theresa Müller-Gajjar, all of whom have supported my endeavours over the years and helped me to develop into the person I am today. I also wish to acknowledge my friend, Robert Jones, who made me feel so at home following my relocation to Buckinghamshire in England and always giving providing sound advice. I thank my Fortismere work colleagues, Sarah Ogilby, Mellany Topping, Fiona Collins and Edward Jeffries. Finally special thanks are extended to my dear friends, Willie Möller, Burke Christian, and housemate, Professor David Craig, with whom I have enjoyed many academic conversations whilst partaking in good food and the odd glass of wine.

The above lesson will encourage self discipline and aural development. Active participation is crucial for the development of skills as outlined in the Aims and Objectives and highlighted in the Lesson Plan. Homework will be assigned – see Log Book.

Mario Maxwell Müller – Lesson Plan presented for the Qualification:
Licentiate in Music Teaching (LRSL) – MUS T601

As part of your course you have to submit a video recording demonstrating each level with either a group or individual lesson

- **Level 1 – Group Teaching (Rosie and Ella) – Grade 1 – DVD1**
- **Level 2 - Candidate's performance – Grade 4 – DVD2**
- **Level 3 – Individual teaching (Tibor) – Grade 8 – DVD3**

Repertoire:
Level 1 – Rosie and Ella
Musical Piece: Ten-to-Ten by Tim Richards
Supplementary material: Trinity Guildhall Piano Initial Pieces and exercises,
Additional work set from: Associated Board of the Royal Schools of Music Grade 1 and Grade 2 theory books.

Level 2 – Candidate's performance
Musical Piece: Raised on the Gospel by Tim Richards

Level 3 – Tibor
Musical Piece: Silent Movie Chase by Debbie Wiseman
Sight-reading: Christmas Lullaby by John Rutter
Supplementary material: Trinity Guildhall Piano Grade 8 piano pieces and exercises,
Additional work set from: Associated Board Royal Schools of Music Grade 7 and 8 theory books.

The above lesson will encourage self discipline and aural development. Active participation is crucial for the development of skills as outlined in the Aims and Objectives and highlighted in the Lesson Plan. Homework will be assigned – see Log Book.

Mario Maxwell Müller – Lesson Plan presented for the Qualification:
Licenciate in Music Teaching (LRSL) – MUS T601

rockschool

STUDENT PRACTICE LOG BOOK

Name of Student: _____

Date/ Week No: _____   Lesson Time: _____

Arpeggios/ Exercises: _____

Pieces: _____

Other Work: _____

Teacher's Comments: _____   Poor/ Satisfactory/ Good/Excellent

Practice	Mon	Tue	Wed	Thurs	Fri	Sat	Sun	Signature
Scales, Arpeggios and Exercises.								
Pieces								
Total Practice								

Student's/ Parent's Comments: _____

The above lesson will encourage self discipline and aural development. Active participation is crucial for the development of skills as outlined in the Aims and Objectives and highlighted in the Lesson Plan. Homework will be assigned – see Log Book.

Mario Maxwell Müller – Lesson Plan presented for the Qualification:
Licentiate in Music Teaching (LRSL) – MUS T601

rockschool

20 Week Lesson Plans for Grade 1 – Level 1

The above lesson will encourage self discipline and aural development. Active participation is crucial for the development of skills as outlined in the Aims and Objectives and highlighted in the Lesson Plan. Homework will be assigned – see Log Book.

Mario Maxwell Miller – Lesson Plan presented for the Qualification:
Licentiate in Music Teaching (LRSL) – MUS T601

rockschool

	Week 1	Week 2	Week 3	Week 4	Week 5	Week 6	Week 7	Week 8	Week 9	Week 10
					10 Week Plan					
Performance:	Choo-Choo Train Boogie		Ten-to Ten		In the Red Feeling Blue		Just One More Chance	Ariapeta Avenue	Cat and Mouse	Preparation for Examination
Music Theory/ Notation:	Semibreve, Minims, Crotchets, Quavers including rest / Accidentals (Sharp, Natural and flats) / Key signature: G Maj	Dynamic Markings: Piano – soft / Mezzo Forte - Moderately loud / Forte – Loud / Time signature: 4/4	Recognition of Pitches on the Treble and bass clef / Note values / Tied notes / Key signature: C Maj	Recognition of Letter names of Treble and Bass clef / Note value – rests/ / Time signature: 4/4	Key signatures / Fermata (Pause)	Time signatures / Fermata (Pause)	Dotted crotchets / Tied notes / Fermata (Pause)	Time signature: 2/2 / Forte – loud / Syncopated notes	Time signature: ¾ / Forte – Loud / Piano – soft / Tied notes / Dotted minim	Major and Minor Tonic Chords in Root position. / Pitch Recognition / Note Values / Dynamics
Scales and Exercises:	C Maj Scale for Right and Left Hand.	A – Aeolian Scale for Right and Left Hand.	C Maj (Pentatonic) 3 Note Pattern for Right and Left Hand.	E Min (Pentatonic) 3 Note Pattern for Right and Left Hand.	G Major Broken Chord for Right and Left Hand.	A Minor Broken Chord for Right and Left Hand.	First three Scales for Right and Left Hand. / C Maj Scale / A – Aeolian / C Maj (Pentatonic) with 3 note pattern.	Next three scales for Right and Left Hand. / E min (Pentatonic) with 3 note pattern. / G Maj Broken Chord / A Min Broken Chord	All scales to date for right and left hand	All scales to date for both right and left hand.
Ear Tests:	Test 1a – P12	Test 1b- P13	Test 1c – P13	Test 1d – P13	Test 1e – P13	Test 2 a – P13	Test 2b –P13	Test 2c – P13	Test 2d – P13	Test 2e – P13
Technique:	Staccato, Boogie feeling	Staccato, Tempo change, steady beat	How to play legato and tied notes. Staccato.	Walking Bass lines, Dynamics and Tied notes.	Dynamics, Phrasings, Articulation	Syncopated Rhythms	Steady beat and tempo to enhance performance.	Syncopation, contrast of legato and Staccato.	Intro to Dorian mode, phrasings and articulations	Syncopation, Legato, Staccato, Steady beat.
Sight Reading:	Bar 1 of SR Test P 12	Bar 2 of SR Test P12	Bar 3 of SR Test P12	Bar 4 of SR Test P12	Improvisation Chord Amin P 12	Improvisation Chord F Maj P12	Improvisation Chord C Maj P12	Improvisation Chord G Maj P12	Whole Sight reading test P12	Whole Improvisation test P 12

The above lesson will encourage self discipline and aural development. Active participation is crucial for the development of skills as outlined in the Aims and Objectives and highlighted in the Lesson Plan. Homework will be assigned – see Log Book.

Mario Maxwell Müller – Lesson Plan presented for the Qualification:
Licentiate in Music Teaching (LRSL) – MUS T601

rockschool

Music Practical (Lesson 1 - Piano) – GROUP LESSON

Age: Varied
Skills: Working towards Grade1
Time: 20 Minutes

Keywords: **C major Scale - Right Hand, Staccato, Flat, Natural and Sharp**
Piano, Mezzo forte, Forte, Time signature, Key signature, Semibreve, Minim, Crotchet, Quaver
Rest (Semibreve, Minim, Crotchet and Quaver), correct posture when performing on piano.

Resources: Piano, Rock School Grade 1 Piano Book, Pencil, Music Stand, Manuscript Paper, Practice Log Book and Metronome.

Lesson Aims:	Listening Test (Aural), Sight-reading, Technical Exercises, Student will play prescribed piece – Grade 1 and Theory.
Lesson Objectives:	• Students will start with the **Music Notation** on Page 3.
	• Student need to play an ascending and descending **C Major scale** using the correct fingering (slight underneath and cross over) for right hand only on Page 3.
	• Students will sight read bar 1 on Page 12 (focussing on chromatic C to C sharp notes).
	• Students will start working on **Choo- Choo Train Boogie** by Adrian York – First play the right hand and then the left hand until bar 8.
	• Students will familiar themselves with the **musical terms** including **piano**, **mezzo forte**, **forte**, **and accelerando** with reference to bar 3 and the **tempo change** in bar 5.
	• Students will need to differentiate between a quaver, crotchet and quaver rest.
	• Students will familiar themselves with the G Major scale in preparation for ear training test 1 (a) on page 13 - focussing on using the crotchet notes from the G major scale using notes G, A and B

Lesson Plan

Time:	Lesson Content	Teaching Methods	Assessment Methods
2 Minutes	The teacher will introduce the Music notation as illustrated on page 3 focussing on the musical staff, grace notes, and how to play the music note staccato on the piano.	Illustration, discussion and demonstration.	Students will demonstrate.
3 Minutes	The teacher will introduce the C major scale using the correct hand position for the right hand with the correct fingering. Especially the slighting action underneath within the scale ascending and cross over action with the scale descending. The students will play two octaves as indicated on page 3.	Demonstration and discussion.	Students will demonstrate.
12 Minutes	The teacher will perform the first musical piece until bar 8. The students will play only the right hand until bar 8. Using the correct rhythm, staccato and musical notes and correct accidentals being played. Students will know how to play a sharp and natural of any given note on the piano. Then the students will play the left hand using the correct rhythm and musical notes especially A sharp until bar 8.	Demonstration, illustration and discussion.	Students will demonstrate and perform musical piece using both hands.
3 Minutes	The teacher will ask the students to play the first bar of the sight reading test on p 12. The teacher will play the G Maj scale and ask the students to play back the melody (p 13).	Demonstration and discussion	Sight reading test with ear test – Students will demonstrate.

The above lesson will encourage self discipline and aural development. Active participation is crucial for the development of skills as outlined in the Aims and Objectives and highlighted in the Lesson Plan. Homework will be assigned – see Log Book.

Mario Maxwell Müller – Lesson Plan presented for the Qualification:
Licentiate in Music Teaching (LRSL) – MUS T601

Music Practical (Lesson 2 - Piano) – GROUP LESSON

Age: Varied

Keywords: C major Scale - Left Hand. Staccato, Flat, Natural and Sharp

Skills: Working towards Grade1

Piano, Mezzo forte, Forte, Time signature, Key signature, Semibreve, Minim, Crotchet, Quaver

Time: 20 Minutes

Rest (Semibreve, Minim, Crotchet and Quaver), correct posture when performing on the piano.

Resources: Piano, Rock School Grade 1 Piano Book, Pencil, Music Stand, Manuscript Paper, Practice Log Book and Metronome.

Lesson Aims:	Listening Test (Aural), Sight-reading, Technical Exercises, Student will play prescribed piece – Grade 1 and Theory.
Lesson Objectives:	• Students will recap some of the music theory for the **Music Notation** on Page 3.
	• Students need to play an ascending and descending **C Major scale** using the correct fingering (cross over and slight underneath) for left hand only on Page 3.
	• Students will sight read bar 2 on Page 12 (focussing on correct notes being played).
	• Students will continue working on **Choo Choo Train Boogie** by Adrian York - first right hand and then left hand until bar 16.
	• Students need to familiar themselves with the various accidentals and correct fingering as indicated on the piano score.
	• Emphasise students to perform in a **Boogie style.**
	• Students will familiar themselves with the **G Major scale** in preparation for Ear training Test 1 (b) on page 13- focussing on using crotchet notes from the G major scale using G, A and B including Test 2 (a) and clapping the rhythm back.

Lesson Plan

Time:	Lesson Content	Teaching Methods	Assessment Methods
2 Minutes	The teacher recap what was taught in the previous lesson with regard to music theory and re-introduce letter names on the treble and bass clef as part of the music notation on Page 3?	Illustration, discussion and demonstration.	Theory test
3 Minutes	The teacher will introduce C major scale using the correct hand position for the left hand and also using the correct fingering. Especially slighting underneath with scale ascending and cross over with scale descending. Students will play two octaves as indicated on Page 3.	Demonstration and discussion.	Students will demonstrate.
13 Minutes	The teacher will perform musical piece until bar 16. The students will play only the right hand until bar 16. Using the correct rhythm, staccato and musical notes with playing the accidentals. Students will know how to play a sharp and natural note of any given note. Now the students will play the left hand using the correct rhythm, musical notes being aware of the E flat to E natural in bar 10 and correct fingering in bar 13. The teacher will start with ear training Test (2a) on p 13.	Demonstration, illustration and discussion.	Students will demonstrate. Students will perform musical piece with both hands. Ear training test. Students will clap rhythm back after hearing 2 bar melody twice.
2 Minutes	The teacher will ask the students to play second bar as sight reading test on Page 12. Ear test as indicated on 1(b) p 13.	Demonstration and discussion	Sight Reading test with ear test – Students will demonstrate.

The above lesson will encourage self discipline and aural development. Active participation is crucial for the development of skills as outlined in the Aims and Objectives and highlighted in the Lesson Plan. Homework will be assigned – see Log Book.

Mario Maxwell Müller – Lesson Plan presented for the Qualification:
Licentiate in Music Teaching (LRSL) – MUS T601

rockschool

Music Practical (Lesson 3 - Piano) – GROUP LESSON

Age: Varied   Keywords: **A - Aeolian Scale - Right Hand. Staccato, Flat, Natural and Sharp**
Skills: Working towards Grade1   **Piano, Mezzo forte, Forte, Time signature, Key signature, Semibreve, Minim, Crotchet, Quaver**
Time: 20 Minutes   **Rest (Semibreve, Minim, Crotchet and Quaver), correct posture when performing on piano.**
Resources: Piano, Rock School Grade 1 Piano Book, Pencil, Music Stand, Manuscript Paper, Practice Log Book and Metronome.

Lesson Aims:	Listening Test (Aural), Sight-reading, Technical Exercises, Student will play prescribed piece – Grade 1 and Theory.
Lesson Objectives:	• Students will recap some of the music theory as part of the **Music Notation** on Page 3.
	• Students need to play an ascending and descending **A - Aeolian scale** using the correct fingering (slight underneath and cross over) for right hand only on Page 3.
	• Sight read bar 3 and bar 4 on Page 12 (focussing on the correct notes being used).
	• Students will continue working on **Choo Choo Train Boogie** by Adrian York - First the right hand and then left hand until bar 20.
	• Students need to familiar themselves with the various accidentals and correct fingering as indicated on the piano score.
	• Emphasise students to perform in a Boogie style.
	• Students will familiar themselves with the G Major scale in preparation for Ear training Test 1 (c) on page 13- focussing on using crotchet notes from the G Major Scale using G, A and B including Test 2 (b) and clapping the rhythm back.

Lesson Plan

Time:	Lesson Content	Teaching Methods	Assessment Methods
2 Minutes	The teacher recaps what was taught in the previous lesson with regard to music theory and re-introduces letter names on treble and bass clef as part of the music notation on Page 3.	Illustration, discussion and demonstration.	Theory test
3 Minutes	The teacher will introduce A - Aeolian scale using the correct hand position for the right hand and also using the correct fingering. Especially slighting underneath with scale ascending and cross over with scale descending. Students will play two octaves as indicated on Page 3.	Demonstration and discussion.	Students will demonstrate.
13 Minutes	The teacher will perform musical piece until bar 20. The students will play only the right hand until bar 20. Using the correct rhythm, staccato and musical notes with playing the accidentals. Now the students will play the left hand using the correct rhythm, fingering and musical notes until bar 20. The teacher will start with ear training Test 2 (b) on p 13.	Demonstration, illustration and discussion.	Students will demonstrate. Students will perform musical piece using both hands. Ear training test. Students will clap rhythm back after hearing 2 bar melody twice.
2 Minutes	The teacher will ask the students to play third and fourth bar as sight reading test on Page 12. The teacher will play G Maj scale -students will play back melody as indicated on 1(c) p 13.	Demonstration and discussion	Sight reading test with ear test – Students will demonstrate.

The above lesson will encourage self discipline and aural development. Active participation is crucial for the development of skills as outlined in the Aims and Objectives and highlighted in the Lesson Plan. Homework will be assigned – see Log Book.

Mario Maxwell Müller – Lesson Plan presented for the Qualification:
Licentiate in Music Teaching (LRSL) – MUS T601

Music Practical (Lesson 4 - Piano) – GROUP LESSON – DVD 1

Age: Varied   Keywords: **A - Aeolian Scale - Right Hand. Legato, Staccato, Flat, Natural and Sharp.**

Skills: Working towards Grade1   **Mezzo forte, Forte, Pause, Time signature, Key signature, Semibreve, Minim, Crotchet, Quaver**

Time: 20 Minutes   **Rest (Semibreve, Minim, Crotchet and Quaver), correct posture when performing on piano.**

Resources: Piano, Rock School Grade 1 Piano Book, Pencil, Music Stand, Manuscript Paper, Practice Log Book and Metronome.

Lesson Aims:	Listening Test (Aural). Sight-reading. Technical Exercises. Student will play prescribed piece – Grade 1 and Theory.
Lesson Objectives:	• Students will recap some of the music theory as part of **Music Notation** on Page 3.
	• Students need to play an ascending and descending **A - Aeolian scale** using the correct fingering (slight underneath and cross over) for the left hand only on Page 3.
	• Sight read - improvisation ad interpretation bar 1 and bar 2 on P 12 (focussing chords especially A min and F Maj).
	• Students will start working on **Ten- to – Ten** by Tim Richards - first right hand and then left hand until bar 10.
	• Students need to familiar themselves with playing a musical note legato with the various accidentals and correct fingering as indicated on the piano score.
	• Emphasise action in the left hand which imitates the walking bass lines and tied notes.
	• Students will familiar themselves with the G Major scale in preparation for the Ear training Test 1 (d) on page 13 - focussing on using crotchet notes from the G major scale using G, A and B including Test 2 (c) and clapping the rhythm back.

Lesson Plan

Time:	Lesson Content	Teaching Methods	Assessment Methods
2 Minutes	The teacher recap what was taught in the previous lesson with regard to music theory and re-introduce letter names on treble and bass clef as part of the music notation on Page 3?	Illustration, discussion and demonstration.	Theory test
3 Minutes	The teacher will introduce A - Aeolian scale using the correct hand position for the left hand and also using the correct fingering. Especially slighting underneath with scale ascending and cross over with scale descending. Students will play two octaves as indicated on Page 3.	Demonstration and discussion.	Students will demonstrate.
13 Minutes	The teacher will play the second musical piece until bar 10. The students will play only the right hand until bar 10. Using the correct rhythm, musical notes, playing the accidentals and tied notes. Now the students will play the left hand using the correct rhythm, playing legato, correct fingering and musical notes until bar 10. The teacher will start with ear training Test 2 (c) on p 13.	Demonstration, illustration and discussion.	Students will demonstrate. Students will perform musical piece with both hands. Ear training test. Students will clap rhythm back after hearing 2 bar melody twice.
2 Minutes	The teacher will ask the students to play bar 1 and 2 of the Improvisation as sight reading test on P 12. The teacher will play G Maj scale - students will play back melody on 1(d) p 13.	Demonstration and discussion	Sight reading test with ear test – Students will demonstrate.

The above lesson will encourage self discipline and aural development. Active participation is crucial for the development of skills as outlined in the Aims and Objectives and highlighted in the Lesson Plan. Homework will be assigned – see Log Book.

Mario Maxwell Müller – Lesson Plan presented for the Qualification:
Licentiate in Music Teaching (LRSL) – MUS T601

rockschool

Music Practical (Lesson 5 - Piano) – GROUP LESSON*

Age: Varied Keywords: **A - Aeolian Scale – Left Hand. Staccato, Flat, Natural, Sharp and Tied notes.**

Skills: Working towards Grade1 **Mezzo forte, Forte, Time signature, Key signature, Semibreve, Minim, Crotchet and Quaver.**

Time: 20 Minutes **Rest (Semibreve, Minim, Crotchet and Quaver), correct posture when performing on piano.**

Resources: Piano, Rock School Grade 1 Piano Book, Pencil, Music Stand, Manuscript Paper, Practice Log Book and Metronome.

Lesson Aims:	Listening Test (Aural), Sight-reading, Technical Exercises, Student will play prescribed piece – Grade 1 and Theory.
Lesson Objectives:	• Students will recap some of the music theory as part of the **Music Notation** on Page 3.
	• Students need to play an ascending and descending **C major (Pentatonic) scale** using the three note pattern for the right hand only on Page 3.
	• Sight reading - improvisation and interpretation bar 3 and bar 4 on P 12 (focussing chords especially C Maj and G Maj).
	• Students will continue working on **Ten- to – Ten** by Tim Richards - first right hand and then left hand until bar 20.
	• Students need to familiar themselves with playing a musical note legato with accidentals and correct fingering as indicated on the piano score.
	• Emphasise action in the left hand which imitates the walking bass lines and tied notes.
	• Students will familiar themselves with the G Major scale in preparation for Ear training Test 1 (e) on page 13- focussing on using crotchet notes from the G major scale using G, A and B including Test 2 (d) and clapping the rhythm back.

Lesson Plan

Time:	Lesson Content	Teaching Methods	Assessment Methods
2 Minutes	The teacher recap what was taught in the previous lesson with regard to music theory and re-introduce letter names on treble and bass clef as part of the music notation on Page 3?	Illustration, discussion and demonstration.	Theory test
3 Minutes	The teacher will introduce C major (pentatonic) scale using the correct hand position for the right hand and also using the correct fingering. Especially cross over with scale ascending and slighting underneath with scale descending. Students will play two octaves as indicated on Page 3.	Demonstration and discussion.	Students will demonstrate.
13 Minutes	The teacher will play the second musical piece until bar 20. The students will play only the right hand until bar 20. Using the correct rhythm, musical notes, playing the accidentals and tied notes. Now the students will play the left hand using the correct rhythm, playing legato, correct fingering and musical notes until bar 20. The teacher will start with ear training Test 2 (d) on p 13.	Demonstration, illustration and discussion.	Students will demonstrate. Students will perform musical piece using both hands. Ear training test. Students will clap rhythm back after hearing 2 bar melody twice.
2 Minutes	The teacher will ask the students to play bar 3 and 4 of Improvisation as sight reading test on Page 12. The teacher will play G Maj scale - students will play back the melody as indicated on 1(d) p 13.	Demonstration and discussion	Sight reading test with ear test – Students will demonstrate.

The above lesson will encourage self discipline and aural development. Active participation is crucial for the development of skills as outlined in the Aims and Objectives and highlighted in the Lesson Plan. Homework will be assigned – see Log Book.

Mario Maxwell Müller – Lesson Plan presented for the Qualification:
Licentiate in Music Teaching (LRSL) – MUS T601

Music Practical (Lesson 6 - Piano) – GROUP LESSON

Age: Varied **Keywords:** **C Major Pentatonic – Right Hand (3 Note Pattern). Staccato, Flat, Natural, Sharp, Tied notes.**

Skills: Working towards Grade1 **Mezzo forte, Forte, Time signature, Key signature, Semibreve, Minim, Crotchet and Quaver.**

Time: 20 Minutes **Rest (Semibreve, Minim, Crotchet and Quaver), piano and pause sign.**

Resources: Piano, Rock School Grade 1 Piano Book, Pencil, Music Stand, Manuscript Paper, Practice Log Book and Metronome.

Lesson Aims:	Listening Test (Aural). Sight-reading. Technical Exercises. Student will play prescribed piece – Grade 1 and Theory.
Lesson Objectives:	• Students will recap some of the music theory as part of the **Music Notation** on Page 3.
	• Students need to play an ascending and descending **C Maj Pentatonic scale (3 note pattern)** using the correct fingering for the right hand only on Page 3 emphasising the three note pattern.
	• Students will start working on **In the Red Feeling Blue** by Simone Wallace - first right hand and then left hand until bar 10.
	• Students need to familiar themselves with playing a musical note legato and the various accidentals with correct fingering as indicated on the piano score.
	• Emphasise detail of dynamics, phrasing and articulation with emphasis on the syncopated rhythms.
	• Students will familiar themselves with the G Major scale in preparation for Ear training Test 1 (a) on page 13- focussing on using crotchet notes from the G major Scale using G, A and B including Test 2 (a) and clapping the rhythm back.

Lesson Plan

Time:	Lesson Content	Teaching Methods	Assessment Methods
2 Minutes	The teacher recap what was taught in the previous lesson with regard to music theory and re-introduce letter names on treble and bass clef as part of the music notation on Page 3?	Illustration, discussion and demonstration.	Theory test
3 Minutes	The teacher will re-introduce C Maj Pentatonic scale using the correct hand position for the right hand and also using the correct fingering. Especially focussing on three note pattern. Students will play scale as indicated on Page 3.	Demonstration and discussion.	Students will demonstrate.
13 Minutes	The teacher will play the third musical piece until bar 10. The students will play only the right hand until bar 10. Using the correct rhythm, musical notes, playing the accidentals and tied notes. Now the students will play the left hand using the correct rhythm, playing legato, correct fingering and musical notes until bar 10. Teacher will focus on dynamics, articulation and syncopated rhythms. The teacher will start with ear training Test 2 (a) on p 13.	Demonstration, illustration and discussion.	Students will demonstrate. Students will perform musical piece using both hands. Ear training test. Students will clap rhythm back after hearing 2 bar melody twice.
2 Minutes	The teacher will recap the sight reading test on page 12. The teacher will play G Maj scale -students will play back the melody as indicated on 1(a) p 13.	Demonstration and discussion	Sight reading test with ear test – Students will demonstrate.

The above lesson will encourage self discipline and aural development. Active participation is crucial for the development of skills as outlined in the Aims and Objectives and highlighted in the Lesson Plan. Homework will be assigned – see Log Book.

Mario Maxwell Miller – Lesson Plan presented for the Qualification:
Licentiate in Music Teaching (LRSL) – MUS T601

Music Practical (Lesson 7 - Piano) – GROUP LESSON

Age: Varied	Keywords: **C Major Pentatonic – Left Hand (3 Note Pattern)**. **Staccato, Flat, Natural, Sharp, Tied notes.**
Skills: Working towards Grade1	**Mezzo forte, Forte, Time signature, Key signature, Semibreve, Minim, Crotchet and Quaver.**
Time: 20 Minutes	**Rest (Semibreve, Minim, Crotchet and Quaver), piano and pause sign.**

Resources: Piano, Rock School Grade 1 Piano Book, Pencil, Music Stand, Manuscript Paper, Practice Log Book and Metronome.

Lesson Aims:	Listening Test (Aural), Sight-reading, Technical Exercises. Student will play prescribed piece – Grade 1 and Theory.
Lesson Objectives:	• Students will recap some of the music theory as part of the **Music Notation** on Page 3.
	• Students need to play an ascending and descending **C Maj Pentatonic scale (3 note pattern)** using the correct fingering for the left hand only on Page 3 emphasising the three note pattern.
	• Students will continue working on **In the Red Feeling Blue** by Simone Wallace - first right hand and then left hand until bar 19.
	• Students need to familiar themselves with playing a musical note legato and the various accidentals with correct fingering as indicated.
	• Emphasise detail of dynamics, phrasing and articulation with emphasis on syncopated rhythms.
	• Students will familiar themselves with the G Major scale in preparation for Ear training Test 1 (b) on page 13- focussing on using crotchet notes from the G major scale using G, A and B including Test 2 (b) and clapping the rhythm back.

Lesson Plan

Time:	Lesson Content	Teaching Methods	Assessment Methods
2 Minutes	The teacher recap what was taught in the previous lesson with regard to music theory and re-introduce letter names on treble and bass clef as part of the music notation on Page 3?	Illustration, discussion and demonstration.	Theory test
3 Minutes	The teacher will introduce C Maj Pentatonic scale using the correct hand position for left hand and also using the correct fingering. Especially focussing on the three note pattern. Students will play scale as indicated on Page 3.	Demonstration and discussion.	Students will demonstrate.
13 Minutes	The teacher will play the third musical piece until bar 19. The students will play only the right hand until bar 19. Using the correct rhythm, musical notes, playing the accidentals and tied notes. Now the students will play the left hand using the correct rhythm, playing legato, correct fingering and musical notes until bar 19. Teacher will focus on dynamics, articulation and syncopated rhythms. The teacher will start with ear training Test 2 (b) on p 13.	Demonstration, illustration and discussion.	Students will demonstrate. Students will perform musical piece using both hands. Ear training test. Students will clap rhythm back after hearing 2 bar melody twice.
2 Minutes	The teacher will recap the sight reading test on page 12. The teacher will play G Maj scale -students will play back the melody as indicated on 1(b) p 13.	Demonstration and discussion	Sight reading test with ear test – Students will demonstrate.

The above lesson will encourage self discipline and aural development. Active participation is crucial for the development of skills as outlined in the Aims and Objectives and highlighted in the Lesson Plan. Homework will be assigned – see Log Book.

Mario Maxwell Müller – Lesson Plan presented for the Qualification:
Licentiate in Music Teaching (LRSL) – MUS T601

Music Practical (Lesson 8 - Piano) – GROUP LESSON

Age: Varied
Skills: Working towards Grade1
Time: 20 Minutes

Keywords: **E Minor Pentatonic – Right Hand (3 Note Pattern). Staccato, Flat, Natural, Tied notes. Mezzo forte, Forte, Time signature, Key signature, Minim, dotted minim and crotchet. Dotted crotchet and crotchet rest, piano and pause sign (fermata).**

Lesson Aims:	Listening Test (Aural), Sight-reading, Technical Exercises. Student will play prescribed piece – Grade 1 and Theory.
Lesson Objectives:	• Students will recap some of the music theory as part of the **Music Notation** on Page 3.
	• Students need to play an ascending and descending **E Min Pentatonic scale (3 note pattern)** using the correct fingering for the right hand only on Page 3 emphasising the three note pattern.
	• Students will start working on **Just One More Chance** by Terry Seabrook - first right hand and then left hand until bar 10. Students need to familiar themselves with playing a musical note legato and accidentals with correct fingering as indicated on the piano score.
	• Emphasise regular sense of beat and counting 1 & 2 & 3 & 4 with keeping a steady beat to enhance great performance.
	• Students will familiar themselves with the G Major scale in preparation for Ear training Test 1 (c) on page 13- focussing on using crotchet notes from the G major scale using G, A and B including Test 2 (c) and clapping the rhythm back.

Lesson Plan

Time:	Lesson Content	Teaching Methods	Assessment Methods
2 Minutes	The teacher recap what was taught in the previous lesson with regard to music theory and re-introduce letter names on treble and bass clef as part of the music notation on Page 3?	Illustration, discussion and demonstration.	Theory test
3 Minutes	The teacher will introduce E Min Pentatonic scale using the correct hand position for right hand and also using the correct fingering. Especially focussing on three note pattern. Students will play scale as indicated on Page 3.	Demonstration and discussion.	Students will demonstrate.
13 Minutes	The teacher will play the fourth musical piece until bar 10. The students will play only the right hand until bar 10. Using the correct rhythm, musical notes, playing the accidentals and tied notes. Now the students will play the left hand using the correct rhythm, playing legato, correct fingering and musical notes until bar 10. Teacher will focus on dynamics, articulation and counting 1 & 2 & 3 & 4 to maintain a steady beat and express the performance with feeling. The teacher will start with ear training Test 2 (c) on p.13.	Demonstration, illustration and discussion.	Students will demonstrate. Students will perform musical piece using both hands. Ear training test. Students will clap rhythm back after hearing 2 bar melody twice.
2 Minutes	The teacher will recap the sight reading test on page 12. The teacher will play G Maj scale -students will play back the melody as indicated on 1(c) p.13.	Demonstration and discussion	Sight reading test with ear test – Students will demonstrate.

The above lesson will encourage self discipline and aural development. Active participation is crucial for the development of skills as outlined in the Aims and Objectives and highlighted in the Lesson Plan. Homework will be assigned – see Log Book.

Mario Maxwell Müller – Lesson Plan presented for the Qualification:
Licentiate in Music Teaching (LRSL) – MUS T601

Music Practical (Lesson 9 - Piano) – GROUP LESSON

Age: Varied   **Keywords:** **E Minor Pentatonic – Left Hand (3 Note Pattern). Staccato, Flat, Natural, Tied notes.**
Skills: Working towards Grade1   **Mezzo forte, Forte, Time signature, Key signature, Minim, dotted minim and crotchet.**
Time: 20 Minutes   **Dotted crotchet and crotchet rest, piano and pause sign (fermata).**
Resources: Piano, Rock School Grade 1 Piano Book, Pencil, Music Stand, Manuscript Paper, Practice Log Book and Metronome.

Lesson Aims:	Listening Test (Aural), Sight-reading, Technical Exercises, Student will play prescribed piece – Grade 1 and Theory.
Lesson Objectives:	• Students will recap some of the music theory as part of the **Music Notation** on Page 3.
	• Students need to play an ascending and descending **E Min Pentatonic scale (3 note pattern)** using the correct fingering for the left hand only on Page 3 emphasising the three note pattern.
	• Students will continue working on **Just One More Chance** by Terry Seabrook - first right hand and then left hand until bar 20.
	• Students need to familiar themselves with playing a musical note legato with accidentals and correct fingering as indicated on the piano score.
	• Emphasise regular sense of beat and counting 1 & 2 & 3 & 4 with keeping a steady beat to enhance a great performance.
	• Students will familiar themselves with the G Major scale in preparation for Ear training Test 1 (d) on page 13- focussing on using crotchet notes from the G major scale using G, A and B including Test 2 (d) and clapping the rhythm back.

Lesson Plan

Time:	Lesson Content	Teaching Methods	Assessment Methods
2 Minutes	The teacher recap what was taught in the previous lesson with regard to music theory and re-introduce letter names on treble and bass clef as part of the music notation on Page 3?	Illustration, discussion and demonstration.	Theory test
3 Minutes	The teacher will introduce E Min Pentatonic scale using the correct hand position for left hand and also using the correct fingering. Especially focussing on three note pattern. Students will play scale as indicated on Page 3.	Demonstration and discussion.	Students will demonstrate.
13 Minutes	The teacher will play the fourth musical piece until bar 20. The students will play only the right hand until bar 20. Using the correct rhythm, musical notes, playing the accidentals and tied notes. Now the students will play the left hand using the correct rhythm, playing legato, correct fingering and musical notes until bar 20. Teacher will focus on dynamics, articulation and counting 1 & 2 & 3 & 4 to maintain a steady beat and express the performance with feeling. The teacher will start with ear training Test 2 (d) on p 13.	Demonstration, illustration and discussion.	Students will demonstrate. Students will perform musical piece using both hands. Ear training test. Students will clap rhythm back after hearing 2 bar melody twice.
2 Minutes	The teacher will recap sight reading test on page 12. The teacher will play G Maj scale -students will play back the melody as indicated on 1(d) p 13.	Demonstration and discussion	Sight reading test with ear test – Students will demonstrate.

The above lesson will encourage self discipline and aural development. Active participation is crucial for the development of skills as outlined in the Aims and Objectives and highlighted in the Lesson Plan. Homework will be assigned – see Log Book.

Mario Maxwell Müller – Lesson Plan presented for the Qualification:
Licentiate in Music Teaching (LRSL) – MUS T601

Music Practical (Lesson 10 - Piano) – GROUP LESSON

Age: Varied   Keywords: **G Major Broken Chord – Right Hand, Staccato, Tied notes.**
Skills: Working towards Grade1   **Forte, Time signature, Key signature, Crotchet and Quaver.**
Time: 20 Minutes   **Rests (Crotchet and Quaver)**
Resources: Piano, Rock School Grade 1 Piano Book, Pencil, Music Stand, Manuscript Paper, Practice Log Book and Metronome.

Lesson Aims:	Listening Test (Aural), Sight-reading, Technical Exercises, Student will play prescribed piece – Grade 1 and Theory.
Lesson Objectives:	• Students will recap some of the music theory as part of the **Music Notation** on Page 3.
	• Students need to play an ascending and descending **G Maj Broken Chord** using the correct fingering for the right hand only on Page 3.
	• Students will start working on **Ariapeta Avenue** by Mark Cherrie - first right hand and then left hand until bar 10.
	• Students need to familiar themselves with playing a musical note legato and the various accidentals with correct fingering as indicated.
	• Emphasise the syncopation with reference to bar 3, 4, 6 and 8 where the right hand anticipates the left.
	• Students will familiar themselves with the G Major scale in preparation for Ear training Test 1 (e) on page 13- focussing on using crotchet notes from the G major scale using G, A and B including Test 2 (e) and clapping the rhythm back.

	Lesson Plan		
Time:	Lesson Content	Teaching Methods	Assessment Methods
2 Minutes	The teacher recap what was taught in the previous lesson with regard to music theory and re-introduce letter names on treble and bass clef as part of the music notation on Page 3?	Illustration, discussion and demonstration.	Theory test
3 Minutes	The teacher will introduce G Maj broken chord scale using the correct hand position for the right hand and also using the correct fingering. Students will play scale as indicated on P 3.	Demonstration and discussion.	Students will demonstrate.
13 Minutes	The teacher will play the fifth musical piece until bar 10. The students will play only the right hand until bar 10. Using the correct rhythm and musical notes. Now the students will play the left hand using the correct rhythm, playing legato, correct fingering and musical notes until bar 10. Teacher will focus on syncopation especially bars 3, 4, 6 and 8 where the right hand anticipates the left. Bringing each hand together slowly and in time. Teacher will also make students aware of the rhythm of the last bar: 1, 4, 6 and 7 with explaining contrasts between legato and staccato. The teacher will start with ear training Test 2 (e) on p 13.	Demonstration, illustration and discussion.	Students will demonstrate. Students will perform musical piece using both hands. Ear training test. Students will clap rhythm back after hearing 2 bar melody twice.
2 Minutes	The teacher will recap sight reading test on page 12. The teacher will play G Maj scale -students will play back the melody as indicated on 1(e) p 13.	Demonstration and discussion	Sight reading test with ear test – Students will demonstrate.

The above lesson will encourage self discipline and aural development. Active participation is crucial for the development of skills as outlined in the Aims and Objectives and highlighted in the Lesson Plan. Homework will be assigned – see Log Book.

Mario Maxwell Müller – Lesson Plan presented for the Qualification:
Licentiate in Music Teaching (LRSL) – MUS T601

Music Practical (Lesson 11 - Piano) – GROUP LESSON

Age: Varied   Keywords: **G Major Broken Chord – Left Hand, Staccato, Tied notes.**

Skills: Working towards Grade1   **Forte, Time signature, Key signature, Crotchet and Quaver.**

Time: 20 Minutes   **Rests (Crotchet and Quaver)**

Resources: Piano, Rock School Grade 1 Piano Book, Pencil, Music Stand, Manuscript Paper, Practice Log Book and Metronome.

Lesson Aims:	Listening Test (Aural), Sight-reading, Technical Exercises, Student will play prescribed piece – Grade 1 and Theory.
Lesson Objectives:	• Students will recap some of the music theory as part of the **Music Notation** on Page 3.
	• Students need to play an ascending and descending **G Maj Broken Chord** using the correct fingering for the left hand only on Page 3.
	• Students will continue working on **Ariapeta Avenue** by Mark Cherrie - first right hand and then left hand until bar 20.
	• Students need to familiar themselves with playing a musical note legato and the various accidentals with correct fingering as indicated.
	• Emphasise the syncopation with reference to bar 3, 4, 6 and 8 where the right hand anticipates the left.
	• Students will familiar themselves with the G Major scale in preparation for Ear training Test 1 (a) on page 13- focussing on using crotchet notes from the G major scale using G, A and B including Test 2 (a) and clapping the rhythm back.

Lesson Plan

Time:	Lesson Content	Teaching Methods	Assessment Methods
2 Minutes	The teacher recap what was taught in the previous lesson with regard to music theory and re-introduce letter names on treble and bass clef as part of the music notation on Page 3?	Illustration, discussion and demonstration.	Theory test
3 Minutes	The teacher will introduce G Maj broken chord scale using the correct hand position for left hand and also using the correct fingering. Students will play scale as indicated on P.3.	Demonstration and discussion.	Students will demonstrate.
13 Minutes	The teacher will play the fifth musical piece until bar 20. The students will play only the right hand until bar 20. Using the correct rhythm, musical notes, accidentals and tied notes. Now the students will play the left hand using the correct rhythm, playing legato, correct fingering and musical notes until bar 20. Teacher will focus on syncopation especially bars 3, 4, 6 and 8 where the right hand anticipates the left. Bringing each hand together slowly and in time. Teacher will also make students aware of the rhythm of the last bar: 1, 4, 6 and 7 with explaining contrasts between legato and staccato. The teacher will start with ear training Test 2 (a) on p.13.	Demonstration, illustration and discussion.	Students will demonstrate. Students will perform musical piece using both hands. Ear training test. Students will clap rhythm back after hearing 2 bar melody twice.
2 Minutes	The teacher will recap sight reading test on page 12. The teacher will play G Maj scale -students will play back melody as indicated on 1(a) p.13.	Demonstration and discussion	Sight reading test with ear test – Students will demonstrate.

The above lesson will encourage self discipline and aural development. Active participation is crucial for the development of skills as outlined in the Aims and Objectives and highlighted in the Lesson Plan. Homework will be assigned – see Log Book.

Mario Maxwell Müller – Lesson Plan presented for the Qualification:
Licentiate in Music Teaching (LRSL) – MUS T601

rockschool

Music Practical (Lesson 12 - Piano) – GROUP LESSON

Age: Varied
Skills: Working towards Grade1
Time: 20 Minutes
Resources: Piano, Rock School Grade 1 Piano Book, Pencil, Music Stand, Manuscript Paper, Practice Log Book and Metronome.

Keywords: **A Minor Broken Chord – Right Hand, Staccato, Tied notes.**
Piano, Forte, Time signature, Key signature, Crotchet, dotted crotchet, minim, dotter minim.
Quaver note Rests (Semibreve and Crotchet)

Lesson Aims:	Listening Test (Aural), Sight-reading, Technical Exercises, Student will play prescribed piece – Grade 1 and Theory.
Lesson Objectives:	• Students will recap some of the music theory as part of **Music Notation** on Page 3.
	• Students need to play an ascending and descending and descending **A Minor Broken Chord** using the correct fingering for the Right Hand only on Page 3.
	• Students will start working on **Cat and Mouse** by Janette Mason - First Right hand and then Left hand until Bar 10.
	• Students need to familiar themselves playing both hands simultaneously and using the correct fingering as indicated.
	• Emphasise use of phrasings, articulation and dynamics.
	• Students will familiar themselves with the G Major scale in preparation for Ear training Test 1 (b) on page 13- focussing on using crotchet notes from the G Major Scale using G, A and B including Test 2 (b) and clapping the rhythm back.

Lesson Plan

Time:	Lesson Content	Teaching Methods	Assessment Methods
2 Minutes	The teacher recap what was taught in the previous lesson with regard to music theory and re-introduce letter names on treble and bass clef as part of the music notation on Page 3?	Illustration, discussion and Demonstration.	Theory test
3 Minutes	The teacher will introduce A min broken chord scale using the correct hand position for Right Hand and also using the correct fingering. Students will play scale as indicated on P 3.	Demonstration and discussion.	Students will demonstrate.
13 Minutes	The teacher will play the sixth musical piece until bar 10. The students will play only the right hand until bar 10. Using the correct rhythm, musical notes, playing the tied notes. Now the students will play the left hand using the correct rhythm, fingering and musical notes until bar 10. Teacher will focus on phrasings, articulation and dynamics. The teacher will start with ear training Test 2 (b) on p 13.	Demonstration, illustration and discussion.	Students will demonstrate. Students will perform musical piece using both hands. Ear training test. Students will clap rhythm back after hearing 2 bar melody twice.
2 Minutes	The teacher will recap sight reading test on page 12. The teacher will play G Maj scale -students will play back melody as indicated on 1(b) p 13.	Demonstration and discussion	Sight reading test with ear test – Students will demonstrate.

The above lesson will encourage self discipline and aural development. Active participation is crucial for the development of skills as outlined in the Aims and Objectives and highlighted in the Lesson Plan. Homework will be assigned – see Log Book.

Mario Maxwell Müller – Lesson Plan presented for the Qualification:
Licentiate in Music Teaching (LRSL) – MUS T601

Music Practical (Lesson 13 - Piano) – GROUP LESSON

Age: Varied   Keywords: **A Minor Broken Chord – Left Hand, Staccato, Tied notes.**

Skills: Working towards Grade1   **Piano, Forte, Time signature, Key signature, Crotchet, dotted crotchet, minim, dotter minim.**

Time: 20 Minutes   **Quaver note Rests (Semibreve and Crotchet)**

Resources: Piano, Rock School Grade 1 Piano Book, Pencil, Music Stand, Manuscript Paper, Practice Log Book and Metronome.

Lesson Aims:	Listening Test (Aural), Sight-reading, Technical Exercises. Student will play prescribed piece – Grade 1 and Theory.
Lesson Objectives:	• Students will recap some of the music theory as part of the **Music Notation** on Page 3.
	• Students need to play an ascending and descending **A Minor Broken Chord** using the correct fingering for the left hand only on Page 3.
	• Students will start working on **Cat and Mouse** by Janette Mason - first right hand and then left hand until bar 20.
	• Students need to familiar themselves playing both hands simultaneously and using the correct fingering as indicated.
	• Emphasise use of phrasings, articulation and dynamics.
	• Students will familiar themselves with the G Major scale in preparation for Ear training Test 1 (c) on page 13- focussing on using crotchet notes from the G major scale using G, A and B including Test 2 (c) and clapping the rhythm back.

Lesson Plan

Time:	Lesson Content	Teaching Methods	Assessment Methods
2 Minutes	The teacher recap what was taught in the previous lesson with regard to music theory and re-introduce letter names on treble and bass clef as part of the music notation on Page 3?	Illustration, discussion and demonstration.	Theory test
3 Minutes	The teacher will introduce A min broken chord scale using the correct hand position for left hand and also using the correct fingering. Students will play scale as indicated on P.3.	Demonstration and discussion.	Students will demonstrate.
13 Minutes	The teacher will play the sixth musical piece until bar 20. The students will play only the right hand until bar 20. Using the correct rhythm, musical notes, playing the tied notes. Now the students will play the left hand using the correct rhythm, fingering and musical notes until bar 20. The teacher will focus on phrasings, articulation and dynamics and the use of the right hand fingering three bars from the end. The teacher will start with ear training Test 2 (c) on p.13.	Demonstration, illustration and discussion.	Students will demonstrate. Students will perform musical piece using both hands. Ear training test. Students will clap rhythm back after hearing 2 bar melody twice.
2 Minutes	The teacher will recap sight reading test on page 12. The teacher will play G Maj scale -students will play back melody as indicated on 1(c) p.13.	Demonstration and discussion	Sight reading test with ear test – Students will demonstrate.

The above lesson will encourage self discipline and aural development. Active participation is crucial for the development of skills as outlined in the Aims and Objectives and highlighted in the Lesson Plan. Homework will be assigned – see Log Book.

Mario Maxwell Müller – Lesson Plan presented for the Qualification:
Licentiate in Music Teaching (LRSL) – MUS T601

Music Practical (Lesson 14 - Piano) – GROUP LESSON

Age: Varied **Keywords: Revision of note values, time signatures and recognition of pitches, dynamic markings.**
Skills: Working towards Grade1 **All the rests, Key signatures, Pause (Fermata)**
Time: 20 Minutes
Resources: Piano, Rock School Grade 1 Piano Book, Pencil, Music Stand, Manuscript Paper, Practice Log Book and Metronome.

Lesson Aims:	Listening Test (Aural), Sight-reading, Technical Exercises, Student will play prescribed piece – Grade 1 and Theory.
Lesson Objectives:	• Students will recap all the music theory as part of the **Music Notation** on Page 3.
	• Students will start playing two sets of scales for right and left hand – **C major and A – Aeolian Scale.**
	• Students will perform two pieces using both hands simultaneously using the correct fingering as indicated for **Choo Choo Train Boogie and Ten-to-Ten.**
	• Students need to express themselves musically using the correct phrasings, articulation and dynamics.
	• Students will complete two Ear- training Tests namely Tests 1 (a) and 1 (b).
	• Students will clap back the rhythm of the two bar melody after hearing it played twice namely Tests 2 (a) and 2 (b).

Lesson Plan

Time:	Lesson Content	Teaching Methods	Assessment Methods
2 Minutes	The teacher will recap on all the elements of music including pitch recognition and various letter names and position for Treble and Bass clef on the Piano.	Illustration, discussion and demonstration.	Theory test
3 Minutes	The teacher will ask students to play C Major and A – Aeolian scale using the correct fingering for right and left hand only – two octaves.	Demonstration and discussion.	Students will demonstrate.
13 Minutes	The teacher will ask students to perform two musical pieces namely Choo Choo Train Boogies and Ten-to Ten using the correct tempo, rhythm and musical notes focussing on phrasings, dynamics and articulation. Teacher will reaffirm boogie style with the sense of an old stream train gradually picking up speed. Students will perform Choo Choo Train Boogie and Ten-to Ten on the piano. Student will demonstrate expressing walking bass lines that the left hand imitates. Students will perform Ear training test using prescribed Tests 2(a) and 2 (b).	Demonstration, illustration and discussion.	Students will demonstrate. Students will perform musical piece using both hands. Ear training test. Students will clap rhythm back after hearing 2 bar melody twice.
2 Minutes	The teacher will ask students to play the complete sight reading test on P 12. Teacher will request students to play back melody consisting of notes using the G major scale and only crotchets (G, A and B) Test 1 (a) and (b).	Demonstration and discussion	Sight reading test with ear test – Students will demonstrate.

The above lesson will encourage self discipline and aural development. Active participation is crucial for the development of skills as outlined in the Aims and Objectives and highlighted in the Lesson Plan. Homework will be assigned – see Log Book.

Mario Maxwell Müller – Lesson Plan presented for the Qualification:
Licentiate in Music Teaching (LRSL) – MUS T601

Music Practical (Lesson 15 - Piano) – GROUP LESSON

Age: Varied   Keywords: **Revision of note values, time signatures and recognition of pitches, dynamic markings.**

Skills: Working towards Grade1   **All the rests, Key signatures, Pause (Fermata)**

Time: 20 Minutes

Resources: Piano, Rock School Grade 1 Piano Book, Pencil, Music Stand, Manuscript Paper, Practice Log Book and Metronome.

Lesson Aims:	Listening Test (Aural), Sight-reading, Technical Exercises. Student will play prescribed piece – Grade 1 and Theory.
Lesson Objectives:	<ul><li>Students will recap all the music theory as part of the **General Musicianship.**</li><li>Students will start playing two sets of scales for Right and Left hand – **C Major Pentatonic and E minor Pentatonic (using three note patterns).**</li><li>Students will perform two pieces using both hands simultaneously and using the correct fingering as indicated for **In the Red Feeling Blue and Just One more Chance.**</li><li>Students need to express themselves musically using the correct phrasings, articulation and dynamics.</li><li>Students will complete two Ear- training Tests namely Tests 1 (c) and 1 (d).</li><li>Students will clap back the rhythm of the two bar melody after hearing it played twice namely Tests 2 (c) and 2 (d).</li></ul>

Lesson Plan

Time:	Lesson Content	Teaching Methods	Assessment Methods
2 Minutes	The teacher will recap on all elements of music including pitch recognition and various letter names and position for Treble and Bass clef on the Piano.	Illustration, discussion and Demonstration.	Theory test
3 Minutes	The teacher will ask students to play C Major and E Minor Pentatonic scale using the correct fingering for the right and left hand.	Demonstration and discussion.	Students will demonstrate.
13 Minutes	The teacher will ask students to perform two musical pieces namely In the Red Feeling Blue and Just One More Chance using the correct tempo, rhythm and musical notes focussing on phrasings, dynamics and articulation with syncopated rhythms and keeping a steady beat with reference to Just One More Chance. Students will perform musical pieces on the piano. Students will perform Ear training test using prescribed Tests 2(c) and 2 (d).	Demonstration, illustration and discussion.	Students will demonstrate. Students will perform musical piece using both hands. Ear training test. Students will clap rhythm back after hearing 2 bar melody twice.
2 Minutes	The teacher will ask students to play the complete sight reading test on P 12. Teacher will request students to play back melody consisting of notes using the G major scale and only crotchets (G, A and B) Test 1 (a) and (b).	Demonstration and discussion	Sight reading test with ear test – Students will demonstrate.

The above lesson will encourage self discipline and aural development. Active participation is crucial for the development of skills as outlined in the Aims and Objectives and highlighted in the Lesson Plan. Homework will be assigned – see Log Book.

rockschool

Mario Maxwell Miller – Lesson Plan presented for the Qualification:
Licentiate in Music Teaching (LRSL) – MUS T601

Music Practical (Lesson 16 - Piano) – GROUP LESSON

Age: Varied Keywords: **Revision of note values, time signatures and recognition of pitches, dynamic markings.**
Skills: Working towards Grade1 **All the rests, Key signatures, Pause (Fermata)**
Time: 20 Minutes
Resources: Piano, Rock School Grade 1 Piano Book, Pencil, Music Stand, Manuscript Paper, Practice Log Book and Metronome.

Lesson Aims:	Listening Test (Aural), Sight-reading, Technical Exercises, Student will play prescribed piece – Grade 1 and Theory.
Lesson Objectives:	• Students will recap all the music theory as part of the **General Musicianship.** • Students will start playing two sets of scales for right and left hand – **G Major and A Minor Broken Chords.** • Students will perform two pieces using both hands simultaneously and using the correct fingering as indicated for **Ariapeta Avenue and Cat and Mouse.** • Students need to express themselves musically using the correct phrasings, articulation and dynamics. • Students will complete one Ear- training Test namely Test 1 (e). • Students will clap back the rhythm of the two bar melody after hearing it played twice - Tests 2 (e).

Lesson Plan

Time:	Lesson Content	Teaching Methods	Assessment Methods
2 Minutes	The teacher will recap on all elements of music including pitch recognition and various letter names and position for Treble and Bass clef on the Piano.	Illustration, discussion and demonstration.	Theory test
3 Minutes	The teacher will ask students to play G Major and A Minor Broken Chords using the correct fingering for right and left hand.	Demonstration and discussion.	Students will demonstrate.
13 Minutes	The teacher will ask students to perform two musical pieces namely Ariapeta Avenue and music piece Cat and Mouse using the correct tempo, rhythm and musical notes focussing on phrasings, dynamics and articulation. With reference to Ariapeta creating a contrast between legato and staccato, Students will perform musical pieces on the piano. Students will perform Ear training test using prescribed Test 2 (e).	Demonstration, illustration and discussion.	Students will demonstrate. Students will perform musical piece using both hands. Ear training test. Students will clap rhythm back after hearing 2 bar melody twice.
2 Minutes	The teacher will ask students to play the complete sight reading test for improvisation on Page 12. Teacher will request students to play back melody consisting of notes using the G major scale and only crotchets (G, A and B) Test 1 (e).	Demonstration and discussion	Sight reading test with ear test – Students will demonstrate.

The above lesson will encourage self discipline and aural development. Active participation is crucial for the development of skills as outlined in the Aims and Objectives and highlighted in the Lesson Plan. Homework will be assigned – see Log Book.

Mario Maxwell Müller – Lesson Plan presented for the Qualification:
Licentiate in Music Teaching (LRSL) – MUS T601

Music Practical (Lesson 17 - Piano) – GROUP LESSON
Age: Varied   Keywords: **Revision of note values, time signatures and recognition of pitches, dynamic markings.**
Skills: Working towards Grade 1   **All the rests, Key signatures, Pause (Fermata) Root position – Major.**
Time: 20 Minutes
Resources: Piano, Rock School Grade 1 Piano Book, Pencil, Music Stand, Manuscript Paper, Practice Log Book and Metronome.

Lesson Aims:	Listening Test (Aural), Sight-reading, Technical Exercises, Student will play prescribed piece – Grade 1 and Theory.
Lesson Objectives:	• Students will recap all the music theory as part of the **General Musicianship.**
	• Students will play all scales up to date (C Maj, A – Aeolian, C Maj and E Min (Pentatonic), G Maj and A min (Broken Chords) – right hand only.
	• Students will choose three pieces to perform at student concert in preparation for their examinations.
	• Students need to express themselves musically using the correct phrasings, articulation and dynamics.
	• Students will complete 5 Ear- training Tests namely Tests 1 (a) – (e).
	• Students will play all prescribed major chords in root position.

Lesson Plan

Time:	Lesson Content	Teaching Methods	Assessment Methods
2 Minutes	The teacher will recap on all elements of music focussing how a major chord is written starting with root, a 3rd and a perfect 5th.	Illustration, discussion and demonstration.	Theory test.
4 Minutes	The teacher will ask students to play all scales up to date starting with C Maj, A – Aeolian, C Maj and E Min (Pentatonic), G Maj and A Min Broken Chords for the right hand only.	Demonstration and discussion.	Students will demonstrate.
10 Minutes	The teacher will ask students to choose their favourite three pieces that students will perform at student concert in preparation for their examination. Students will play Tonic Chord of Major Scales in root position only.	Demonstration, illustration and discussion.	Students will demonstrate. Students will perform musical piece using both hands.
4 Minutes	The teacher will ask students to play sight reading test first and then play back the melody using G Major Scales and notes including (G, A and B). The prescribed Tests 1(a) – (e) will be used.	Demonstration and discussion	Sight reading test with ear test – Students will demonstrate. Students will play back the five different melodies heard.

The above lesson will encourage self discipline and aural development. Active participation is crucial for the development of skills as outlined in the Aims and Objectives and highlighted in the Lesson Plan. Homework will be assigned – see Log Book.

Mario Maxwell Müller – Lesson Plan presented for the Qualification:
Licentiate in Music Teaching (LRSL) – MUS T601

Music Practical (Lesson 18 - Piano) – GROUP LESSON

Age: Varied   Keywords: **Revision of note values, time signatures and recognition of pitches, dynamic markings.**
Skills: Working towards Grade1   **All the rests, Key signatures, Pause (Fermata) Root position – Minor.**
Time: 20 Minutes
Resources: Piano, Rock School Grade 1 Piano Book, Pencil, Music Stand, Manuscript Paper, Practice Log Book and Metronome.

Lesson Aims:	Listening Test (Aural), Sight-reading, Technical Exercises, Student will play prescribed piece – Grade 1 and Theory.
Lesson Objectives:	• Students will recap all the music theory as part of the **General Musicianship.**
	• Students will play all scales up to date (C Maj, A – Aeolian, C Maj and E Min (Pentatonic), G Maj and A min (Broken Chords) – left hand only.
	• Students will choose three pieces to perform at student concert in preparation for their examinations.
	• Students need to express themselves musically using the correct phrasings, articulation and dynamics.
	• Students will complete 5 Ear- training Tests namely Tests 2 (a) – (e) and clap back the rhythm.
	• Students will play all prescribed minor chords in root position.

Lesson Plan

Time:	Lesson Content	Teaching Methods	Assessment Methods
2 Minutes	The teacher will recap on all the elements of music focussing how a minor chord is written starting with root, a minor 3rd and a perfect 5th.	Illustration, discussion and demonstration.	Theory test.
4 Minutes	The teacher will ask students to play all scales up to date starting with C Maj, A – Aeolian, C Maj and E Min (Pentatonic), G Maj and A Min Broken Chords for the left hand only.	Demonstration and discussion.	Students will demonstrate.
11 Minutes	The teacher will ask students to choose their favourite three pieces that students will perform at student concert in preparation for their examination. Focus of the lesson will be on musicality and interpretation of the musical piece. Students will play Tonic Chord of Minor Scales in root position only.	Demonstration, illustration and discussion.	Students will demonstrate. Students will perform musical piece using both hands.
3 Minutes	The teacher will ask students to play sight reading test and clap back the rhythm of the following five Ear tests from Tests 2 (a) – (e).	Demonstration and discussion	Sight reading test with ear test – Students will demonstrate.

The above lesson will encourage self discipline and aural development. Active participation is crucial for the development of skills as outlined in the Aims and Objectives and highlighted in the Lesson Plan. Homework will be assigned – see Log Book.

Mario Maxwell Müller – Lesson Plan presented for the Qualification:
Licentiate in Music Teaching (LRSL) – MUS T601

Music Practical (Lesson 19 - Piano) – GROUP LESSON

Age: Varied   Keywords: **Revision of note values, time signatures and recognition of pitches, dynamic markings.**

Skills: Working towards Grade1   **All the rests, Key signatures, Pause (Fermata) Root position – Minor.**

Time: 20 Minutes

Resources: Piano, Rock School Grade 1 Piano Book, Pencil, Music Stand, Manuscript Paper, Practice Log Book and Metronome.

Lesson Aims:	Listening Test (Aural). Sight-reading, Technical Exercises. Student will play prescribed piece – Grade 1 and Theory.		
Lesson Objectives:	• Students will recap all the music theory as part of the **General Musicianship.** • Students will play all scales up to date (C Maj, A – Aeolian, C Major Pentatonic using both left and right hands only. • Students will discuss what makes a great performance. • Students need to express themselves musically using the correct phrasings, articulation and dynamics. • Students will complete 5 Ear- training Tests namely Tests 2 (a) – (e) and clap back the rhythm. • Students will play all prescribed major and minor chords in root position.		

Lesson Plan

Time:	Lesson Content	Teaching Methods	Assessment Methods
2 Minutes	The teacher will recap on all elements of music focussing how a major and minor chord is written and ask student to write down prescribed chords.	Illustration, discussion and demonstration.	Theory test.
4 Minutes	The teacher will ask students to play all scales up to date starting with C Maj, A – Aeolian and C Maj (Pentatonic) scales using right and left hand only.	Demonstration and discussion.	Students will demonstrate.
11 Minutes	The teacher will discuss what makes a great performance and test students on general musician questions with reference to three pieces chosen for the practical examination. The teacher will focus on expressions, correct posture, articulation, dynamics and being confident when performing. Students will play Tonic Chord of Major and Minor Scales in root position only.	Demonstration, illustration and discussion.	Students will demonstrate. Students will perform musical piece using both hands.
3 Minutes	The teacher will ask students to play sight reading tests and asked students with reference to all the Ear Tests including playing back melodies, and clapping back the rhythm of a two bar melody.	Demonstration and discussion	Sight reading test with ear test – Students will demonstrate.

The above lesson will encourage self discipline and aural development. Active participation is crucial for the development of skills as outlined in the Aims and Objectives and highlighted in the Lesson Plan. Homework will be assigned – see Log Book.

Mario Maxwell Müller – Lesson Plan presented for the Qualification:
Licentiate in Music Teaching (LRSL) – MUS T601

Music Practical (Lesson 20 - Piano) – GROUP LESSON

Age: Varied   Keywords: **Revision of note values, time signatures and recognition of pitches, dynamic markings.**
Skills: Working towards Grade1   **All the rests, Key signatures, Pause (Fermata) Root position – Minor.**
Time: 20 Minutes
Resources: Piano, Rock School Grade 1 Piano Book, Pencil, Music Stand, Manuscript Paper, Practice Log Book and Metronome.

Lesson Aims:	Listening Test (Aural), Sight-reading, Technical Exercises. Student will play prescribed piece – Grade 1 and Theory.
Lesson Objectives:	• Students will recap all the music theory as part of the **General Musicianship.** • Students will play all scales up to date - right and left hand. • Students will discuss what makes a great performance and correct posture and hand position when playing the piano. • Students need to express themselves musically using the correct phrasings, articulation and dynamics. • Students will complete 5 Ear- training Tests namely Tests 2 (a) – (e) and clap back the rhythm. • Students will play all prescribed major and minor chords in root position.

Lesson Plan

Time:	Lesson Content	Teaching Methods	Assessment Methods
2 Minutes	The teacher will recap on all elements of music focussing how a major and minor chord is written and ask student to write down prescribed chords.	Illustration, discussion and demonstration.	Theory test.
4 Minutes	The teacher will ask students to play all scales up to date starting with E Min (Pentatonic), G Maj and A min (Broken Chords) scales using right and left hand only.	Demonstration and discussion.	Students will demonstrate.
11 Minutes	The teacher will discuss what makes a great performance and test students on general musician questions with reference to three pieces chosen for the examination. The teacher will focus on expressions, correct posture, articulation, dynamics and being confident when performing. Correct hand position when performing and playing the piano. Students will play Tonic Chord of Major and Minor Scales in root position only.	Demonstration, illustration and discussion.	Students will demonstrate. Students will perform musical piece using both hands.
3 Minutes	The teacher will ask students to play sight reading test and perform all the Ear Tests including playing back melodies, and clapping back the rhythm of a two bar melody.	Demonstration and discussion	Sight reading test with ear test – Students will demonstrate.

The above lesson will encourage self discipline and aural development. Active participation is crucial for the development of skills as outlined in the Aims and Objectives and highlighted in the Lesson Plan. Homework will be assigned – see Log Book.

Mario Maxwell Müller – Lesson Plan presented for the Qualification: Licentiate in Music Teaching (LRSL) – MUS T601

References:

Pitt, S., York A. & York, N. 2001a. *Grade 1 – Popular Piano and Keyboard Book.* United Kingdom : Rock School Ltd [Internet] < http://www.rockschool.co.uk/books/piano/ > [Accessed June 2010]

Pitt, S., York A. & York, N. 2001b. *Grade 2 - Popular Piano and Keyboard Book.* United Kingdom: Rock School Ltd: [Internet] < http://www.rockschool.co.uk/books/piano/ > [Accessed June 2010]

Pitt, S., York A. & York, N. 2001c. *Grade 3 - Popular Piano and Keyboard Book.* United Kingdom: Rock School Ltd: [Internet] < http://www.rockschool.co.uk/books/piano/ > [Accessed June 2010]

You can obtain the following books referenced in the lesson plans on the following websites:

Websites:

http://www.musicroom.com/rockschool/

The above lesson will encourage self discipline and aural development. Active participation is crucial for the development of skills as outlined in the Aims and Objectives and highlighted in the Lesson Plan. Homework will be assigned – see Log Book.